THROUGH THE EYES OF

The
Cookie
Lady

CRENSHAW & SLAUSON SOUTH CENTRAL LA

VMH Publishing
Atlanta, GA

Copyright © 2019 by Vanessa WilliamS

VMH Publishing
3355 Lenox Rd. NE Ste 750 Atlanta, GA 30326
www.vmhpublishing.com

All rights reserved.

This book may not be reproduced in whole or in part, in any form or by means, electronic or mechanical, including photocopying, recording, or by any information storage and retrieval system now known or hereafter invented, without permission from the publisher.

Bulk Ordering Information:

Quantity sales. Special discounts are available on quantity purchases by corporations, associations, and others. For details, contact the publisher at the address above or via email at: info@vmhpublishing.com

Book Cover Design: VMH Publishing
Cover Image: Shutterstock
Interior Layout: VMH Publishing

Hardback ISBN: 978-1-947928-64-0
Paperback ISBN: 978-1-947928-63-3

Made in United States of America

10 9 8 7 6 5 4 3 2 1

THROUGH THE EYES OF

The Cookie Lady

CRENSHAW & SLAUSON SOUTH CENTRAL LA

Vanessa Williams

My Story

My name is Vanessa, a.k.a. "The Cookie Lady". I sold cookies and cakes at the Slauson Swapmeet for over 18 years and I would always write in my diary the different things that would happen during the time I was there. I was born and raised in South Central Los Angeles right off of 59th Street and Crenshaw. I grew up in the 'Rolling Sixties' neighborhood. Back then I thought it was the baddest gang around; let my brother tell it. He was always saying, "Rolling Sixty Crip," which was a term he coined based off of the neighborhood where we stayed. I lived in a house with my mother, father, older sister, and brother. Being the baby was always a challenge -- it was like being an only child sometimes. My brother and sister were always with their friends, so I was always with my mom. I enjoyed cooking in the kitchen with her. Sweets were my specialty. Every weekend she would make some kind of dessert, and I was always there to help and sample it. I also had my own Easy Bake oven and pans to go with it, so my mom would always make sure to save me some batter from her cakes to put in my pans to bake on my own.

I would love to decorate the cakes and cookies that I made. That was something that kept me busy on the weekend. Then sometimes my friends would come over, since they lived right across the street in Dorset Village. They would help me eat all the cakes or cookies I made for that weekend. They would always tell me how delicious they were. We all went to Hyde Park Elementary School back then. We would walk to school together in the morning and they would always ask me if I was making more cakes and cookies on the weekend.

By the time I got to Audubon Jr. High School, my love for baking kind of slowed down. I started to play basketball that year, which didn't last very long. The next year I attended John Muir Jr. High. It was at that time I really left the baking to my mom. I became too busy with my friends going to the mall on the weekends. Y'all remember the Fox Hills Mall? That mall was everything back then. It was the perfect hangout for me and my friends and we had lots of fun. Back then I only had a couple of dollars, but it was always enough to get what I wanted. The "Hot Dog On The Stick" was one of my favorite spots to eat at. Of course I would hit up the cookie spot as well, as if I didn't already eat enough sweets. We also loved the attention we got from the young men up there.

Every time my friends and I went out we would always exchange numbers with some nice-looking guys, and at times, some not-so-nice-looking ones. In that case, we would give a wrong number out. Then we would hope and pray we didn't run into that guy the next weekend. I've had friends get cussed out for this. Teenage life had its ups and downs.

When I was fifteen years old, I had just graduated from John Muir Jr. High when my dad died. I was devastated. I remember just staying in the house that summer every day. My mom would come home from work and just go to her room. It had to be the worst summer ever. That same year I attended the famous Crenshaw High School. I was starting high school with no dad, and I was afraid of starting this momentous chapter in my life without his wisdom and guidance.

I remember going shopping every weekend with my mom to spend time with her. I think she just didn't know what to do, so she figured if she bought me clothes and shoes that it would distract me from the pain and hurt I was feeling. The loss of my dad really was tough for our family. I guess my mom really felt sorry for me and felt the need to protect or shelter me in some way, since I was the baby.

The first year in high school was tough. As children we are resilient, so I was able to go to school and make good grades with no problem. Coming home, however, always felt sad knowing my dad wasn't going to be there. I could feel my mom's grief every day when she came home from work. Her spirit was just different. She didn't cook like she used to anymore. Her joy went away.

My mom was a cook at the children's center back in the day. I'd always thought she was the best cook ever. Since she didn't cook at home too much, she would bring food home every day instead. I couldn't wait to see what was on the stove when I got home from school. Food was always a source of comfort for me. One day she came home with a cookie recipe and said she would try it out on the weekend. I was shocked since she hadn't baked in so long. But she made these chocolate chip cookies and baby let me tell you -- they were the bomb!

I told her I could sell these at my school. Since she was a single parent, I figured I could help create another source of income. I remember my boyfriend at the time, Suga Will, had come over that day and I was like, "taste these." He tried them and replied, "Omg! These cookies are delicious." So, my mom made a small batch of cookies for me to sell. I took them to school and baby, they were an instant hit. That's when I became known as the 'cookie lady'!

The Cookie Lady

I would take cookies to school every morning. I started off with a batch of 30. Then I would bring 50. I would sell out everyday. I eventually brought 100 a day. I had a friend that lived around the corner from me named Shana. She would help me carry the cookies when my mom dropped us off at school in the morning; she would get one bag and I would get the other. I did really well with my little business. It helped me out a lot in my senior year.

    I was really digging being an entrepreneur, as I always had money in my pocket. When I graduated and went on to attend California State University, I would still go back to Crenshaw High School and sell my cookies after classes. For me it was easy money because I liked baking, and I can thank momma Rosa for that. When I attended college, I was more so baking them for myself. I got really creative and experimental then. I would add more flavors to the menu like oatmeal raisin, peanut butter, or sugar cookies, and I would add things like coconut flakes or almonds.

I remember that same year my cousin, Sean, came to visit me from Georgia. He couldn't believe I baked my own cookies and sold them at the high school. The first time he went with me to Crenshaw High he stayed in the car and watched. Next thing he knew, two young guys nearby pulled out guns and started shooting. Students were running around everywhere and screaming. Of course, Sean panicked and looked for me, saying all he saw was me running haphazardly with the box of cookies. When I finally made it back to the car I looked at him and started laughing. I told him, "welcome to my world." My cousin gave me a serious look and told me it was too dangerous out here to be selling cookies. I tried to tell him that was the first time that happened since I'd been coming after school and he needn't worry.

However, I eventually stopped going up to Crenshaw High shortly after the shooting happened and I started selling cookies elsewhere. I would sell them at the County Building, or sometimes the check cashing places. I would also go to different festivals around town.

I loved to go to the African Market Place by Dorsey High School every year. The atmosphere was amazing. While I was out there selling cookies I would listen to the sound of the African drummers. There were people out there burning tons of sage, so the energy was always peaceful. Children were running around having fun. Everyone out there was on the hustle, trying to get people to buy their products. As for me, I did pretty well for myself there. I would have to go back and forth to the car to reload on the cookies because I would sell out every time.

My Cookies & Slauson Swapmeet

One day I was at the Slauson Swapmeet. I thought to myself, *this would be a great place to sell my cookies on the weekend because it was always crowded.* So, I worked it out with the Slauson Swapmeet's management team. I would come every weekend and sell cookies. Soon after that, I expanded my repertoire as a baker and would make cakes as well. I made this amazing walnut coconut bar and people would always ask me if it was old-school coffee cake. I would answer, "No, no, no." After so many 'no's' I decided to start making the LAUSD (Los Angeles Unified School District) Old School Coffee Cake. I also made this bomb lemon cake, and mastered brownies with walnuts in them. I would make '7-Up' pound cake that would quickly sell out. Sometimes I would even make my all-time favorite cake, German Chocolate, putting extra pecans in it. That cake would go quickly as well. Sometimes I would even do rum and raisin cookies. I would do all this baking and by the time I got to the swapmeet I would just relax and sell my sweets. In between sales, I would always have my diary at the ready. I loved to write. It was therapeutic for me. It was also a good place to keep record of all the daily occurrences/drama that happened while I was there. You wouldn't believe the things that went on at theswapmeet. This is a story straight out of my diary:

This story takes place at the Slauson Swapmeet, taken straight out of my diary I've been writing in for years. Thisswapmeet is centered in the middle of South Central LA. This is a place where everyone loves to come shop or at least visit. They come from different cities, states, and sometimes different countries. The young, old, rich, poor, and handicapped all have come to browse or buy. We even get celebrities that come through sometimes. I would just sit back and observe it all while selling my delicious cookies and cakes. I was the Cookie Lady, baby! I would sit right by the front entrance and observe everything that comes through that door as well as the parking lot.

This is my story. Monday through Friday I taught at the children centers, where I was a substitute for many years. Then on the weekend, I would sell my cookies and cakes. Throughout the week I would stock up on my baking supplies. I would usually get started on Thursday, sometimes Friday, depending on how many cookies and cakes I was baking that weekend. I was usually up half the night and into the early morning baking my delicious pastries to take to theswapmeet. I would load up my Tahoe and off I went. I would always get a parking space up front because I was already tired and not trying to walk far. Some people would say I had an easy job since I just sat there and sold cookies, but they didn't have a clue how much work I put into it. I would load up my little red wagon and get my table together so I could sell my desserts. I always had my pouch attached securely around my waist so no one could potentially snag my money and run off. Thankfully, I'd usually be surrounded by LA's finest security, Diamond Security.

These guys were the most hardworking, exhilarating, and intriguing group of officers you could ever imagine. We had our own police force ready to serve and protect merchants and customers. No one dared to come there using fake credit cards, or with plans to rob jewelry or clothing stores and get away scot-free.

However, that didn't stop people from trying to get away with it. We had petty thieves all day long. They would attempt to steal earrings, hair bows, purses, shirts, etc.

Sometimes the Koreans vendors would run after thieves stealing their merchandise. I've seen them try to fight the thieves to get their stuff back. There was one Korean family who really got aggressive, especially the daughter. She would run up in the thieve's face and argue with them about the items they stole. I said to myself, *one day she will get in the wrong persons face and she will get her ass beat.* Thankfully, the security officers would always arrive on the scene before things escalated further.

Then we had the jewelry thieves. Some guys have gotten away with thousands of dollars' worth of 10k gold jewelry over the years. They'd ask to see an expensive chain and then take off running. Most usually didn't make it that far before they got caught. The security would chase your ass all the way home to get that jewelry back!

People would always target the jewelry store by the front door. I'd be selling my cookies and cakes, minding my own business and boom! They'd take off out the door and once they hit that side gate, they'd be gone. A lot of times they would strike early in the morning when everyone was half asleep, since the response and reaction time was slower.

From time to time we would have big gang fights. There were so many different gangs that shopped at the Slauson. They liked to get t-shirts made in the back where they did the embroidery and airbrushing. Whenever one of their homeboys died, they would get a t-shirt or something made with the name of their gang to honor them. But some would come there looking for trouble and they usually found it. They would run into a gang they didn't like and the arguing would begin. A lot of them were dangerous and would oftentimes pull out guns, so sometimes I had to duck behind something to avoid getting shot by stray bullets. We've had so many shootouts up there over the years, though it has gotten a lot better. They know Diamond Security isn't playing with them.

I remember one time I was on the ramp and the security officers were escorting this young lady out of the mall. She had got caught stealing, so she had to wait outside for her friends to come out. In the meantime, about six guys were walking up the ramp. Then the woman decided she wanted to throw up gang signs at them. Next thing I know, all the guys were up in her face arguing with her. The security officer on the ramp attempted to break up the fight and told the men to leave. Next thing I knew, the sound of gunshots rang through the air. These guys went back to their cars and started shooting at the lady they were arguing with on the ramp. I had to hide inside behind the counter. I didn't think they were ever going to stop. I was so confused about why they didn't make this lady leave in the first place in order to prevent all this trouble, because now innocent people were at risk of getting caught in the crossfire. No one got hurt, thank God.

Every now and then, someone would get robbed in the parking lot or get their car stolen. I've even seen drug deals go bad in the parking lot and some guys have lost their lives over it. I guess they figured the parking lot was so crowded, no one would notice their illicit activities.

One event in particular scarred me for life. I actually watched this one guy die in the parking lot. It had to have been a drug deal gone bad. They just took whatever from him and shot him. We all ran over there to see who got shot and the shooters hopped in the car and got away. People started praying over the man on the ground. I said a little prayer myself. Next thing you know, he stopped breathing and he was gone. It was an eerie thing to witness. I was sad for the rest of the day.

This swapmeet is like a day club. Sometimes you would see brothers or sisters walking in here with drinks in their hand (I called it false courage in a cup). Mostly it was the guys. The women came in half dressed, leaving nothing to the imagination. I would just shake my head. Security would have to always get involved with the guys that had a little too much to drink. They were always harassing the women up there. Security would say, "You ain't gotta go home, but you better get the hell up out of here."

We had Diamond Security's head man, "Big Tony," in charge. He was tall, brown-skinned, had a muscular build, and *fine*. All the ladies loved them some Tony. He had a charming personality when it suited him. He would receive several phone numbers daily. I've watched women slide him their numbers on a piece of paper and he would tuck them in his pocket. I wonder if his wife ever knew about that secret pocket.

Then, there was Eric. He was the sergeant. He reminded me of "Popeye The Sailor Man." It was because of his big, muscular arms and the way he wore his hair. Eric was fine too, but he was the ruthless one. He just didn't give a damn and he would let you know it. He was married as well. But he loved his Latina women. He kept about two or three young Latina girlfriends. They loved them some Eric, probably because he showered them with gifts. You could tell he was a hardcore gangster back in the day. He got excited any time something happened at the swapmeet. He was always ready.

Eric drove the nicest cars. Every last one of them was fixed up. Even his wife's car. They were always clean and looked like they just came out of a showroom. And he always took up two parking spaces near the front ramp to make sure no one scratched his cars. When people would walk up the ramp, they'd be like, "Damn, that's a nice car." And then they'd look at me and ask if it was mine. I would respond jokingly, "Of course it is!"

So, these two men head up security at the Slauson Swapmeet. These guys are ex- gang members, so game recognizes game. They don't play at all. Sometimes other officers find it hard to work with them, so they quit. They can't handle the pressure. But as for me, I loved these guys. They were like my big brothers from another mother, aside from the wild thoughts I had in my head about Big Tony. I know he's married, though, so big brother it stays.

It's early Saturday morning and I roll up to the swapmeet. I try to get there early so I can get my parking space up front. The doors have just opened to let the long-awaited crowd inside. However, we would have people coming in smelling like they hadn't been home to wash their ass, as if they were partying all night and nothing else. Their breath smelled like shit (no offense). Their clothes would also be all wrinkled and stained. Maybe they came in to buy a new outfit for the day. I knew guys that came in there every day just to buy a new t-shirt to wear for that day. I would ask myself, *Don't they ever wash their clothes?* One guy told me he would use the old t-shirts to wash his cars with. Momma Korea must've been rich selling all those t-shirts.

On the side of the ramp there were these guys that hooked up car stereos. They worked for the Korean guy inside. Most of these guys were from Belize. They hooked up car alarms and sound systems all day long. Greg was the main man in charge of installations. He was super friendly if you know what I mean, like extra lovey-dovey. He was a sweetheart though. But this man would come to work like he just rolled out of bed. He would have crust in his eyes, and his t-shirt would be wrinkled. He had long hair that was never combed and a beard that was not lined up. And then there was Winston. He was short, brown-skinned, and sexy. This man had the nicest feet I had ever seen on a man. He loved to wear his sandals and for good reason. He would always talk with me on the ramp while waiting for customers. We were so silly together and would laugh about everything. A lot of times we would just look at each other and laugh because we could read each other's mind.

Sometimes when I left the swapmeet in the evening, Winston would come pick me up from my house later that night to go to a Belizean party. We would party almost every weekend with his other friends. There was always a party somewhere. We would have so much fun. The Sundays after would be so exhausting for me. I was the only one that had to get up and bake that morning, so you know that didn't last very long. Winston and I became good friends over the years, and Greg ended up getting his own stereo shop somewhere else, which I thought was smart of him. If you're going to work that hard it might as well be for yourself.

A lot of times when I arrived at the swapmeet, Big Tony would come out there with his cup of coffee to talk to me. He would always have on these dark-colored sun glasses, trying to hide those tired eyes. I knew exactly how he felt. He usually worked all night and would be super exhausted. I thought highly of the security officers who pulled overnighters. But I guess if you want that money you have to put in the hours.

So, Big Tony and I were talking about random stuff and a couple of guys came up with their pants sagging down. They're not going for that at the Slauson. Big Tony would say, "Pull your pants up, chief!" They kept walking. Big

Tony would tell them again and add, "No entry unless you pull them up." Them knuckleheads kept on walking! Big Tony got on the radio and called for backup. A couple of security officers ran over and they all had to wrestle with these guys and handcuff them and take them to the back.

When things finally settled down, it was time to start selling cookies again. When something is going on, people are nosy and they want to know what's happening; they're not thinking about buying no cookies! But now, here came the Slauson Swapmeet's 'Regulars.' That's what we would call this group of guys that came there every day. They would hang out at the mall all day long. I often wondered if they had jobs.

One of the regulars was named Deshawn. Deshawn would come in everyday with a black bag in his hands to make him look like he's shopping. Sometimes I wanted to just go and grab his bag and run just to be funny. He had a long ponytail and all the women knew him - some in a good way and some in a bad way. The problem with Deshawn is that he would talk to women and then the *friends* of those same women! Guess what would happen all the time? He got cussed out by them, especially when he went to ask for their digits. They'd say, "You just asked for my friend's digits with your thirsty ass." Maybe he liked getting cursed out, or just didn't care. He wanted to hit everything moving. Then we have Big Tony debating if his ponytail is real or not. He would always try to pull it and Deshawn would swat his hand away. Deshawn says he is a music producer. Okay! He must be a broke one. Who knows, maybe he was an undercover millionaire trying to find the right woman. At least he buys cookies from me every weekend and holds on to the bag all day, bless his heart.

We also had another guy that would come through. He was a player as well. He caught the bus almost every day to go to the swapmeet. Sadly, this dude was paralyzed. He rode around with a board that he used as a communication device. He used to be a gangbanger and he ended up getting shot, leaving him paralyzed. Whoever took care of him, though, kept him dressed neatly. His khakis were always perfectly ironed. He always had on fresh, clean tennis shoes. His hair was always braided. I admired his determination to enjoy life in spite of his challenges. He'd always be in here chasing women down for their digits. He probably got more numbers than the other regulars too, to be honest.

    This man would get people he knew, including myself, to call the numbers for him. I never knew how he did it. And he would have money in his pocket! He'd ask me to call these random ladies about giving him a bath. It was so awkward for me. I'd be like, "Hi, C-rock wants to know if you can give him a bath tonight?" It got to the point where I had to tell him to get someone else to do it. It was just so weird what he had going on with these women. Maybe he was paying them, who knows.

I also loved passing the time talking to my other friend, Derrick. A lot of times, he'd be on my ramp. He was also one of Slauson's finest security officers. He has been here forever. He's an OG. He was also just a single brother searching for love. He wasn't quite my type, so that's why I considered him to be more like my big brother, and I probably wasn't his type, either. I could talk to him about anything going on in my life and I didn't have to hear it again, if you know what I mean, and vice versa. We would often stand on the ramp and just talk about people when there wasn't much going on. It made the time go by faster. Derrick hated working at the swapmeet. He would always say, "I can't wait till I get out of here!" He's been trying to leave for years. Unfortunately, sometimes we get stuck in certain jobs and it's hard to find something new. I would always tell him, "One day you will find something better, but if you leave I won't have anyone to laugh and joke with." We could talk about people for hours. There were so many interesting people that walked in and out of those doors. Sometimes I thought the Captain noticed Derrick and I having too much fun, because he would call for an early rotation (meaning they would send him to another door).

One day Derrick and I were on the ramp talking about songs from the eighties. He only listened to oldies. Then he got a call on the radio. A lady was running out of the swapmeet wearing a short skirt with stolen merchandise. She was at full speed, dashing through the cars in the parking lot. A couple of officers were already chasing her when Derrick joined in. The lady was running so fast you would have thought she was a track star. They could barely keep up with her. The officers chased her all the way to the back gate. When there was nowhere else to run, she decided to climb over it. That slowed her down. When the officers grabbed her, they got a big surprise. Her skirt flew up and the family jewels were revealed. It was a man dressed in drag. We all said, "No wonder they could barely catch her, she's a *he*." Guess what he stole? Lingerie! He apparently needed them for a hot date later. That was the excitement for the moment.

About thirty minutes later, Derrick came back on the ramp and here comes a lady walking up with a black fishnet dress on. There was absolutely nothing underneath. To top it off, she was about eight months pregnant. She had to be just a little crazy. Derrick tried to explain to her that they had certain dress codes they went by, and she couldn't go in the swapmeet dressed like that. "Try to stop me," she replied. Then she walked right inside. Derrick had to get on the radio and let the other officers know. He went after the lady to escort her out. People couldn't believe what they were seeing. Derrick had one arm and another man, Lawrence, had the other, all while she was kicking and screaming. *Lord, I hope she doesn't have this baby*, I thought. She ended up punching Lawrence in the face. Hard to believe a pregnant woman had all that strength.

Now Lawrence, a.k.a. 'Action Jackson' or in my book, 'No Action Jackson,' was such a character. The way he walked, you would think he had the biggest bunions on his feet. He'd always complain about his them hurting. He was a middle-aged man with an old body. But hey, he still managed to keep more than one girlfriend. He was a hard working brother, bunions and all, with ten children. He was definitely a family man.

I will never forget the time when Lawrence and Captain Tony were on the ramp together. I noticed a couple of ladies and a big guy fighting. I didn't understand why they would stop in the middle of the parking lot and start fighting. Security was so busy talking that they didn't notice them. So I yelled, "Fight!" and pointed towards the commotion. The funny part was Lawrence ran over there and grabbed the smallest lady there. If only you could've seen the expression on Captain Tony's face when he realized how big the other lady was. She had to be about six feet tall and at least three hundred pounds. He wrestled with her for a long time, trying to put handcuffs on her. Eventually after all the wrestling back and forth, she got away. She hopped in the back seat of her friend's car and popped her on the back of the neck to get her to hurry up and get out of there.

They got away that day. But the security officers did catch the skinny one that Lawrence grabbed. One thing about Lawrence 'Actionless' Jackson was he was not going to make his job hard. He was always trying to take the easy route.

Later that day I asked Lawrence why he didn't grab the other woman. He said, "Girl, are you crazy? You know I have a bad back," he said. "That girl was not about to hurt me." Then he started laughing. Lawrence and I had spent many a day on the ramp laughing about the way he does his job.

Sometimes the LAPD would come up there to see what was going on. We had this one officer that came up there quite often. He would always have a different partner with him. He was an older guy. He actually looked like Barney Fife from The Andy Griffith Show. I remember when I first saw him I thought he was going to tell me I couldn't sell cookies up there. He looked like he was racist. Apparently, I was wrong. He was known throughout the neighborhood. Lawrence said he was cool and married to a black woman. Growing up in the neighborhood, you always thought the worst when you saw the police, but he shocked me. He would always tease me when he came up the ramp. I guess that's why they say to never judge a book by its cover.

Another time we were on the ramp and two different groups of gang bangers walked in. They were throwing up their gang names. They looked like hardcore killers. They had words with each other and then one of them headed to the car. We knew he was going to get a gun. Lawrence got on the radio to call it in. Then he looked at me and asked if my car door was unlocked. He said, "If these damn boys start shooting, I'm hopping in your truck." I said, "Really! Who's going to protect me?" He said, "You better get your ass in the truck, then! I'm too old for this shit." He was always cracking jokes.

I remember another time when Lawrence and I were on the ramp together, and this old couple drove up and parked in the handicap space. They came all the way to the swapmeet to buy some of my famous peanut butter cookies.

The husband said, "My wife said these are the best cookies in the whole wide world." They purchased a couple of packs of cookies and went inside. They probably stayed in the swapmeet for about thirty minutes. In the meantime, parking enforcement arrived. They walked by the older couple's car and noticed there wasn't a handicap sticker. So, they got a ticket. I felt so bad. They placed that bad boy right on the windshield. Lawrence and I looked at each other and shook our heads.

Lawrence said, "When that old man comes out and sees that ticket, he's going to have a heart attack." Eventually they came out. They stopped by again and bought some more cookies to go. *Baby!* Let me tell you! We didn't say a word to them about that ticket. I mean, how do you tell somebody that age that you should know better than to park in a handicap space without a handicap sign? So, when they walked to the car, he opened the door and helped her in like a gentleman would do. As he started walking to the driver's side, he noticed the piece of paper. He started reading that ticket and put his hands over his heart, saying, "Lord Jesus!"

Then he turned to his wife. He said, "I brought your fat ass up here to buy some cookies and I got a three-hundred-and-something dollar ticket! You better not mention anything about these cookies ever again!" Then he clutched his heart again and got in the car. Lawrence ran inside the swapmeet laughing so hard. All I could do was put my head down to keep from doing the same. I guess what made it so funny was that he appeared to be such a gentleman at first, opening up the door for his wife and talking sweetly. And then he saw the ticket and started cursing her out!

I really did feel bad for her. I never saw that couple again. I guess after he got finished paying for that ticket it was a wrap on the cookies. I hope they're still together. She'll probably never hear the end of it.

The next week, Lawrence and I were on the ramp together. We were telling the story to a guy named Chuck. Chuck is another one of the security officers at the Slauson. This dude was *loud!* And *country*! He was from Louisiana. He reminded me of George Jefferson because of his height and short temper. He was also known for cursing everybody out and getting sent home. He would tell the Captain, "You can kiss my ass, I don't need this job!" I thought he was a good officer, but perhaps just misunderstood.

I would love to see Chuck in action. He was an angry black man. He would have to stay on the same ramp all day because he did or said something wrong. The customers would get on his last nerves. After every chase he would come back on the ramp and smoke his cigarettes. As long as Chuck could buy his sex movies from one of the guys at the swapmeet, he was alright. He probably couldn't wait to get home to enjoy them. I believe he was also married with children, if that tells you anything.

He had to be the grumpiest security guard up there, being his country self. I'll never forget the time when Chuck, Melvin, and Clyde were on the ramp making sandwiches on the hood of the car, parked next to the ramp. Clyde went to the store and bought a loaf of bread, sliced ham, cheese, and some mayonnaise. They made some 'hood top' sandwiches. If that ain't country, I don't know what is.

Chuck also liked to come right in your face with a piece of sandwich in his mouth, greasy hands and lips and all, wanting to talk to you. Food would fly everywhere from his mouth as he spoke. That's Chuck all day long.

So, let me tell you about Clyde and Melvin. These guys used to be security guards at the swapmeet back in the day. They traded their badges in for pimp cards. I called them the Diabetic Pimps, since they both had diabetes. They had been friends for years, and they were both married with children. But the way they carried on at the swapmeet, you would think they were single.

Melvin was of average height with a pot belly. He was probably in his fifties, still trying to be a gangster/mack daddy. He swore he was the mack daddy of the year. Whenever he saw a beautiful young woman he'd say, "I think I'm in love, can a brother pay some bills for you?" And you wouldn't believe how many women actually stopped and talked to him. I guess the key phrase was "pay bills."

Clyde, on the other hand, was more comical. He would talk about everybody that walked up the ramp - the way they looked, dressed, and walked. Even though he was the last person that could insult anybody, he still did. However, he had a big heart. He would probably give you the clothes off his back if you needed them.

Melvin and Clyde were definitely "Pimp Daddy Rock Lobsters." I don't know where I got that name from, but it seemed to fit. Whenever Clyde was around Melvin, he automatically turned into a pimp. A soft pimp with a big heart. These two guys were made for each other. Whenever they were around, drama seemed to find them. They made the ramp very entertaining for me.

Clyde would come up to the swapmeet to sell bootleg movies. He had all the latest movies from the theater. Melvin came up there to help him sometimes, and to also admire all the beautiful women. We were all on the ramp one day when two women walked out of the swapmeet. One was short and heavy set, with blonde hair. She reminded me of the lady on the movie, *Bebe's Kids*, with the blonde hair and big butt. Melvin reminded me of the actor, Robin Harris, in that same movie. So, as soon as he sees her, he's on her trail, with their famous saying, "I'm in love like a mutha f...."

Her friend was tall and skinny. That's the one Clyde was looking at. So, of course they exchanged phone numbers. The one with the blonde hair was name Sheila, and her friend's name was Brenda. The Diabetic Pimps were smiling from ear to ear. Melvin was putting that Mack down, showing nothing but teeth. Clyde on the other hand, was showing mostly gums, because a lot of his teeth were missing. After the ladies left, the pimps talked about going on a double date.

So, Melvin and Clyde made plans to pick the ladies up that night. Melvin drove a four-door Cadillac. Clyde drove a Lincoln Continental. Both were pimp daddy cars. I wonder which pimp mobile they ended up driving. I know they were so excited that evening. I guess they forgot they were married with children.

The next day at the swapmeet Melvin and Clyde set up the table full of movies. The day was going great. They were making a lot of money. Sheila and Brenda showed up at the swapmeet that afternoon. Melvin and Clyde were so happy to see them. They gave them some money to go shopping. These guys went from pimps to suckers in no time at all. It was official, they were dating.

And so it began; every day the ladies would come up to the swapmeet to see their boyfriend/sugar daddies and go shopping. They would get their hair done, nails done, etc. I know these ladies thought they came up on some suckers. But who knows, maybe they really liked them. I mean, every single day they came up to the swapmeet. The security knew them. The vendors knew them. They were quite popular up there. It was their every day hang out. I believe they quit their job.

After a while, the men fell head over heels with these women. The hell with their wives and children. The men would do just about anything for them. As time went on, Melvin and Clyde would talk about leaving their wives and moving in with their girlfriends.

They would talk about how their wives treated them. They said they didn't cook or clean the house. They also did not want to work. That's why they knew they would be happier if they left them. But after a while, I guess the wives started to wonder where their husbands were. Every weekend they stayed out late. The men would tell their wives that they were at a low riders convention on the strip. This was a place where all the folks that drove low riders would hang out at night. The low riders were customized cars with hydraulic jacks that allowed the chassis to be lowered close to the ground. The guys would talk and drink and show off their fancy cars.

One day, the wives decided to get dressed and go on the strip where their husbands claim to be at. They drove by all the guys with the low riders. There was no sign of their husbands. They even got out of the car and looked around. There was no sign of them anywhere. They'd been bamboozled. The wives told me they called them on their cellphones. I could hear Melvin now, saying, "Baby you know I'm out here with my boys." And that's exactly what he said.

By now these guys' wives had become suspicious. This shared struggle brought them closer together and brought on a newfound friendship. They started showing up at the swapmeet together. They would ask me questions, but you know me - I don't know nothing, ain't seen nothing, but I hear everything. I remember Clyde saying his famous words, "They up on game like a mutha!" Finally the wives caught them on the ramp with their girlfriends. Baby! Let me tell you, I had to move my table over. I did not want cookies and cakes flying everywhere!

There was all kinds of cursing, screaming, arms flying, pushing, and shoving on the ramp. Melvin tried to grab his wife and Clyde did the same. The wives were beating up them *and* their new girlfriends. I saw blonde hair on the ground, Lord! A loose braid fell from Melvin's wife's head. I stood up and looked for security. I knew this was going to happen. It was just a matter of time.

Finally, the security came running. They got the women under control. These ladies looked like a hot mess. Their wigs were twisted to the side, and nails popped off on the ground. Those wives were so angry that their husbands were cheating on them. Everyone knew they were married; even the girlfriends knew. But they didn't care, as long as they were getting that money. Soon everything was back to normal on the ramp. All the ladies went home.

The next day Clyde said him and Melvin had moved in with their girlfriends, because of course, the wives kicked them out of the house. They said they got home and all their clothes were thrown outside. I thought, *Damn! It seems like they're too old to be going through that shit.* But, you couldn't tell them anything; I guess they enjoyed all the drama. Oh well!

The next weekend at the Slauson Swap meet, everything was going good. The diabetic pimps were back on the ramp selling movies as usual. Next thing I know, the girlfriends were pulling up in new cars thanks to Clyde and Melvin. *These guys must really be sprung*, I thought. Melvin's girlfriend Sheila was driving a white convertible mustang. And Clyde's girlfriend Brenda was driving a red convertible mustang. The movie sells were going great for these guys. I was like *man, they got it going on*. They were making all that money and didn't know what to do with it.

One day we were all on the ramp and people were gathered around Clyde and Melvin buying movies. So, guess who walks in with a white woman on his side, wearing an angry expression, heading straight towards Clyde and Melvin? John Singleton, the film director, screenwriter, producer, and actor. At that time he came out with the movie *Baby Boy* and it was selling like hot cakes. At that point, the ramp sure as hell got quiet. At first, I didn't think Clyde knew who the man was. I believe Melvin did. It was too late to hide the movies. They didn't have any warning of him walking up. I was shocked. I thought, *Oh no!* Everyone had their eyes on John Singleton. Finally he spoke, saying, "Give me all of the copies of my movie right now!" He even asked how many movies were in the car. Well honey, let me tell you, Melvin stepped up and got right up in his face. Melvin told him, "Nigga, you better recognize where the fuck you at, coming up here demanding some movies. I'll rob your ass, take your money, your bitch, *and* your car!"

He also said, "You in the fucking hood nigga, don't get jacked!" Baby! Let me tell you, that man walked away and got on the phone. I don't know who he was calling, but Melvin and Clyde decided to pack up and leave.

We were all on the ramp in disbelief. The security officers came out to see what was going on. They were shocked too that John Singleton himself actually came up to the mall. I think he just came there to look around since he was with a woman and just happened to see someone selling his movies. He did call the police, but by the time they got there, Clyde and Melvin were gone. As for me, I didn't see a thing!

So, the next weekend at the swapmeet Clyde showed up with the movies again. He asked me if the police had been coming around. Of course, I had to let him know what the 411 was. I'm like, "Honey! The police have been up here every day looking for y'all! I guess eventually they just gave up." So, Clyde decided to stand on the ramp and leave his movies in the trunk of his car.

Next thing I knew, here came Melvin and the girlfriends. The guys changed the game up. They let the women stand outside and sell the movies, while they walked around inside, guilt free. And this was the routine every day. The girlfriends were getting all of their money anyway, why not make them earn it? The customers would always ask, "Where are Clyde and Melvin?" The girlfriends would then say, "Around here somewhere." "Letting you do all the work so you'll be the ones who get caught," I would tell them.

One day only Clyde and Brenda came up there to sell movies. Clyde left Brenda outside by herself, while he walked around. She was just selling movies like it was a normal day. Two strange looking guys walked up to her and bought some movies. I had never seen these guys before. Next thing I knew, they were putting her in handcuffs. She was being arrested for selling bootleg movies. I knew they were going to get her.

Clyde saw what was happening and walked around the side of the swapmeet so he didn't get caught. I know he was praying that she didn't snitch on him. Well, of course they asked her where the guy was that she was selling movies for. Brenda told them she didn't know where he was. She even made up a fake name for him. She was not snitching on her man. It astounded me that while Brenda would defend him, he wouldn't do the same for her.

So, they put her in the back seat of the police car. Everyone was outside looking. Derrick and I were just shaking our heads. As the police car was leaving, one of Clyde's friends was walking by. We called him Cupid.

This dummy comes up there from time to time to buy movies from Clyde to resell. He comes up there straight off the bus with a big, black suitcase full of movies. Cupid noticed Brenda in the police car. So, he starts walking along the police car pulling his suitcase. This dummy yells out to the police, "You guys taking her to jail?" Then he tells them, "I'm glad you didn't search me! I have a whole suitcase with movies in it; I dare you to search me!"

Next thing you know the police heard him and stopped the car. They got out of the car and searched this dummy's suitcase. It was full of movies like he said. The police looked at each other and shook their heads. They told Cupid to put his hands behind his back. They put the handcuffs on him and put him in the back of the car with Brenda. Cupid had to have the biggest mouth on that side of town. *And* he went to jail wearing a lime green, pimp daddy suit with finger waves in his hair. Lord have mercy!

I felt bad for Cupid. For someone to be that stupid there had to be something wrong upstairs, if you know what I mean. And this man sold movies to make a living, too. He always came up to the swapmeet with that bus pass hanging from his neck. He usually laid the suitcase between the cars in the parking lot. I don't know what happened that day. I hoped he'd be alright.

Clyde finally came out from hiding. He couldn't believe they just took Brenda and Cupid to jail. I asked him why he didn't come out and say the movies were his so they could let her go. He said with a smirk, "They're not fixin' to take my ass to jail, hell no!" He said that when she called him, he'd go get her out. I asked about his loud-mouth friend. Clyde said to let his big-mouth ass stay in there!

The weekend ended and Monday rolled around. Melvin and Sheila found out about Brenda. Sheila was thankful she wasn't there, because they both would've went to jail. Clyde was waiting for Brenda to call so he could bail her out, but they released her anyway. Clyde felt so bad about her being arrested that he took her and bought her a nice diamond bracelet. And of course she had to come up to the swapmeet to show it off. I guess she had to let everybody know she went to jail for her man!

Another weekend at the swapmeet came. The sun was shining and everybody was out shopping at the Slauson. Melvin finally decided to come back to work selling movies with Clyde. They wanted to make some money. Clyde is a really funny guy. He's always telling jokes all the time. We stay laughing on the ramp. I finally understand what 'dying laughing' means. We'd literally be gasping for air over one of his jokes.

They could have put a show on together called, "The Diabetic Pimps of Comedy."

While we were all sitting on the ramp, Clyde's good buddy, 'Mr. Shine Man', rode up on his bike. He kept all the vendors' cars clean and shiny. This guy's front teeth were messed up. So, of course Clyde and Melvin always liked to clown around with him about his grill. They said he looked like he ate a cement sandwich. We'd all be on the ground in tears, laughing.

Clyde also told us a story about Mr. Shine Man. He said he went to Mississippi to go fishing. When he sat down by the river, a couple of hunters saw him. Clyde said they thought he was a 'coon.' They knocked him in the mouth with a sledge hammer and wrapped him up in a blanket. He said they took him home and sliced some "tatoes and carrots," arranging them around him. Basically, Clyde was saying they took Mr Shine Man home to cook him because they thought he was a raccoon. Clyde was from Mississippi and that's what some people ate over there, apparently.

Everyone on the ramp was laughing so hard that they could barely breath. And Clyde never stopped talking. He saw that we were on the ground already gasping for air, but he would just keep on talking. That was the joke of the day, week, month, and year. Every time we looked at Mr. Shine, we remembered Clyde's story of what happened to his teeth. Sometimes Clyde would switch up the story and use an opossum instead of a coon.

Last year Clyde told everybody that Mr. Shine Man looked like a frozen rat. He said, "Can you imagine opening your freezer and seeing him looking at you? Frozen like a mutha …" Clyde is so silly. Everyone would be on the ramp bent over laughing, tears rolling from people's eyes. If you saw this man, he looked exactly like what Clyde described and that's what made it so funny. Clyde was definitely a comedian.

The next weekend at the swapmeet the parking lot was packed. Each car that passed by had a different beat, some louder than others. You could tell which ones wanted to be seen, with the stereo costing more than the car itself.

Everybody wanted a parking space on the front row. They liked to argue and fight over them as well. This one lady saw this older man waiting for a parking space. I already knew what she was thinking. She probably thought, *this man is old and if I take his spot he's not going to do anything to me.* She decided to swoop in and take the parking space. Oh boy! This man started blowing his horn and the lady did not move. Then, she got out of the car after she pulled into his parking space. He pulled in behind her to block her in. As she walked by his car, the man yelled out, "Lady, I was waiting for that spot!" She said, "So?" She was dressed in a uniform, like she was on her way to work. You could tell he had just come from church, because it was a Sunday and he had on a suit. He yelled back, "Bitch! Move that damn car!" They continued to exchange some choice words.

Finally, after all that, a car pulled out a couple spots down and he parked his car. He got out of the car with his cane. He was a tall, older man with a nice suit on, wearing a hat and nice polished shoes. I have to admit, the man was *clean*. I was on the ramp with Derrick, the security officer that day. The man walked up the ramp and looked over at me and Derrick and said, "The devil sure is busy." And we just looked at each other and laughed. Derrick said, "Damn, he just got out of church and he's cursing like that?"

The lady in uniform rushed out of the swapmeet as if she was late for work. She did take a minute to stop at the end of the ramp to buy some incense from the Incense Prince. This young man sold incense with his father. They both had long dreads, but his father's looked like they'd been growing forever. They were down to the ground. They had the best smelling incense at the swapmeet. You could smell them from a mile away. The young man would also always come to buy my coffee cakes with his sweet-smelling dollar bills. He would have my whole purse smelling good.

I loved the way his father was teaching his son to be an entrepreneur at such a young age. A lot of people passed judgement on his dad because they would stay out there all day, every day. That's how he was making a living for them. It wasn't perfect, but at least he had his son with him every day and was keeping him out of trouble. He went to school, and he looked clean every day. He was also very well-mannered. I think the father was doing a good job raising him.

On another note, we had these other guys come up there every weekend. Kevin, Mario, and Terry were their names. These are the guys that would sit on the ramp and critique every woman that walked by. Sometimes I just stared at these guys and nitpicked all their flaws and thought to myself, *they have some nerve talking about these women that come up here, as if they're perfect people*. They also never came up there to shop; they would just come to hang out.

One day a four-hundred-pound lady walked up the ramp. She had a red G-string showing under her low-cut jeans. Mario looked at her and grabbed his heart. Kevin then replied, "I didn't know elephants wore G-strings." Of course everyone on the ramp started laughing.

These guys usually looked at women's feet, but that g-string took their eyes a little higher. But, mostly they started with the feet. I guess one of the things some guys hated was a woman with dirty feet. They said your feet were the first things that hit the water when you take a shower or bath. They said when they saw a woman with dirty feet, that she obviously didn't wash her ass that day. Kevin said he hated to see women with cute sandals on and dirty feet. It made the whole outfit look bad, according to him.

Another instance was when they'd see a woman walk out of the swapmeet with no shoes on after getting a pedicure. They'd be like, "That's dumb as hell." Mario would say, "Why get your feet cleaned to walk on the nasty ass ground?" I'd respond, "Maybe they just care about their toes being polished." Every weekend there would be something new for them to complain about.

One day I was on the ramp with James. He was also a part of the security team. James was from Mississippi like Clyde. He was just as country as he wanted to be. He would always tease about the Piggly Wiggly's in the south, which are a country grocery store that his grandma and mother shopped at in Mississippi. James is a good looking brother - tall, dark, and sexy, with long legs. The brother was always wearing shorts; it didn't matter what season it was. And I was always crushing on them legs of his. He thought he was a comedian as well. He'd be agreeing with the guys on the ramp that hung out together, talking about the women of course.

James would talk about the times he went to visit different women. He said this one lady was so fine and looked good from head to toe. Then he said he went to go visit her and her house was so nasty that he had to wipe his feet off in the house before he stepped outside. We were all like, "Damn." He said another time he went to visit a young lady and asked to use her bathroom. He said the tub was black as tar. Kevin and Mario would just shake their heads. Mario would then say, "As long as the kitty cat is clean, I'm going in." Really! Sometimes I would get so tired of them talking about women like that, so I would put my headphones on.

These guys had something to say about *everything*. They would talk about bra-less women walking around. They hated to see women without a bra on, coming up there with their breasts hanging to their knee caps. Their breasts would be jumping all around when they walked, and if they hit you, you'd be out for the count. They'd really say stuff like that. Guys nitpick everything about women!

I have heard these guys talk about a lot of stuff you wouldn't even think mattered - like the size of a woman's vagina, the way women smelled down there, the way they looked in the morning, how their shit smelled… like really? It just amazed me how much men criticized women, as if their shit didn't also stink. Like men smell good all the time, when we know they don't. Is their hair neatly cut all the time? Hell no! I see a lot of men with flaws just like women. It got to the point where when I would get ready to go up to the swapmeet, I'd make sure I was on point with everything just so I didn't get talked about. They'd all be like, "Man, did you see Cookie Lady's hair?"

On a funnier note, there was this new security officer. He reminded me of Gomer Pyle from *The Andy Griffith Show*. He was a tall, slender guy. He thought he was the baddest security officer around. He was very arrogant. When he talked he would foam from the mouth. Anytime he would hear a call on the radio, he would be the first one to respond. You know those guys that want to make a name for themselves and they overdo it? That was him.

One time he chased this man all the way across the street to Food Lion. He ran in the grocery store and kicked this man down on the ground, then he handcuffed him. Guess what? The guy he knocked down and handcuffed was an employee there! He handcuffed the wrong guy. The poor employee didn't know what was going on. He thought he was on the show *Candid Camera*. After that incident, I never saw him again. Derrick and I would just laugh at the very conversation of it. They fired his ass real quick. Talk about a liability. Phew!

Another weekend went by and I was on the ramp with Melvin and Clyde again. Derrick was posted on that ramp as well. We saw this guy walking up. He had on some really tight slacks and boots on. You could even see his dick print through his pants! Melvin said, "This nigga using every dick muscle he have to walk up the ramp." We all looked at the front of his pants and started to laugh. We laughed so hard we were almost on the ground. That man looked at us like we were crazy.

We had another officer that worked up there occasionally. His name was Tony. He fixed motorcycles for a living outside of being a security officer. He was also in a motorcycle club. This guy I could never figure out. Sometimes we would talk on the ramp and he would tell me about the women he asked out on dates. He said he would have to let them meet his wife and get her approval. I'd be like, "What?" He said she was okay with it. I guess that meant they had an open relationship. Got it!

Usually when he was working, the wife and kids would come up there. Baby! Let me describe her to you. From the neck up, she looked homey. She wore glasses and her hair was in a bun. From the neck down, she dressed very provocatively. She had a small waist and a huge butt. Everything she wore was super tight and small. She always came up there with their children, too. In my mind, I wondered why a man would allow his wife to dress like this while pushing his children in a stroller? Even though she dressed like a hooker, she was a very nice lady. I just didn't understand her appearance as a married woman.

The men would go crazy looking at this woman walk up the ramp. I have watched guys stop in their tracks just to look at her. She looked like a school teacher from the neck up with her glasses on. Then from the neck down she looked like a hooker. One of the officers coined the term 'swingers.' I'm like, okay! Maybe that explains why she dressed like that. The officer said they would have parties sometimes on the weekend and invite all the security officers. And from a reliable source, they said Tony allowed his wife to perform sex acts on some of the guys. I was astonished. I don't know much about being a swinger, but they could have it. Now every time she came up to the swapmeet I tried not to stare at her. I know everyone makes their own choices in life and a lot of times, it's based on your childhood or something that happened to you. But when I saw this lady and her small children, I really felt sad for her. It's like, what kind of an example are you being for your daughters? Yes, they lived in a nice home. Yes, the children had their dad in their lives, but at what cost? That's why I say I could never figure them out. They looked happy on the outside. I just pray one day that woman realizes her worth.

On a lighter note, we had the maintenance guy, Ricardo. He didn't speak any English, but always wanted to hold a conversation. This guy was an older man. You could tell he was fine back in his younger years, though. He called me "Banessa." He'd always be winking at me. I've known him for years. He'd be in his own little world sometimes, pushing the trash can around, picking up the trash in the parking lot.

One time they had a shootout in the parking lot. One minute you see Ricardo pushing the trash can and the next minute the trash can is all by itself! He'd be next to me, hiding between the cars. I laughed to myself thinking he's always drinking, but I bet that ass sobered up real quick when he heard them gun shots.

When it's all said and done, I wish you could hear Ricardo try to tell the story. He would be so excited that he forgot he didn't speak English and we didn't speak Spanish. We'd all be looking at him like, okay! He also usually had a whole bottle of liquor stashed away somewhere. I could always tell when he was tipsy. He'd make jokes and tell me I was the most beautiful woman in the world, and that he wanted to marry me and take me to Mexico. He said we could "ride on the horse in the sunset." He knew how to say *that* in English. He loved to serenade me.

He was also the same man that would come to work on Christmas Day in a white tuxedo. Okay! He'd be drunk as a skunk. He must have partied all night long and fell asleep in his tux and came straight to work from the party. It was the funniest sight ever. Can you imagine the maintenance man with a broom and dust pan in his hands singing "Feliz Navidad" in his white tuxedo and white shoes? Only at the Slauson, baby! But I love my Ricardo, he keeps me laughing.

Then we had another maintenance man up there, Eduardo. I didn't really care for him. He talked a lot too, but didn't speak English either. He would ask me the same thing over and over. He was more like a pest. He was not funny at all. But he always wanted to talk. I speak and understand some Spanish. I'm not fluent, so I didn't want to have long conversations with him. I'd always be like, "Goodbye, adios!"

Memories

There was another weekend at the Slauson when I was on the ramp with Jesus. Jesus was an older security officer from El Salvador. He used to be a police officer in his country, so sometimes he thought the same rules applied here in America. He did not play games with these people at all. I only saw him smile when he looked at my thighs, calling me his "Mamacita." Every time when we were alone on the ramp together I would have to push his hands away; like really? Can you say, "sexual harassment"? Jesus was an older guy. His wife looked like she was in her fifties and he in his sixties. They were still popping babies out! I've meet some of his children and grandchildren, too. I'd be like, *does this man ever get enough?*

    I loved to watch Jesus in action because like I said, he was serious when it came to his job. I even heard he killed someone up there before. All the gang bangers would come in there and try to disrespect him because of his size and age. They thought they could take him.

I remember one day we were on the ramp and he told this one guy to move his car. The guy ignored him and thought he was still going to come in. Jesus was like, "Go move your car!" And he stood and blocked the entrance so the guy couldn't come in. The guy pushed Jesus out of the way. Wrong move! Jesus flipped his ass over the ramp. A couple of security officers ran over to help him. The guy looked so embarrassed. He said he was going to take them to court. But, you bet he got his ass back in the car and moved it and left. He was limping back to the car and I just laughed. They gonna learn about messing with Jesus.

Later on that day, 'Big Tim' came up on the ramp. Big Tim was a body builder and a body guard who owned his own security company. He did security for a lot of the celebrities. Every time I saw him he had to give me a big bear hug. He had to be about 6'5 and 400 pounds of muscle. I might be over exaggerating, but it seemed like his size to me. He must have used the whole bottle of cologne because I would smell like him for the rest of the day. Usually, Captain Tony would come out to see him on the ramp. He enjoyed taking him to the back to see how much weight he could lift, since Tony lifted as well. I knew Big Tim could probably out-lift them all.

I will always pay my taxes because of Big Tim. He told me the IRS took almost everything he owned. He used to have a nice house and cars, but now he drove up there in an older model car because he had to start over. I don't know why he didn't just pay the taxes and get it over with in the first place. He must have been trying to be cheap. I just didn't understand. To work so hard for these things and just get them taken away must be horrible.

Big Tim loved him some big women, just like Melvin. Except Melvin was paying their bills, and clearly Big Tony wasn't. How could he? He didn't even pay *his* own bills! We'd all be hanging out on the ramp. I'd be selling cookies and they'd be chatting. Big Tim would see a big woman with a big butt and big thighs and he would put his hands on my shoulder, saying, "Lord have mercy!" I guess him being a big guy of 400 pounds, he needed a big woman to match him. I'd say, "Go get her number."

I'll never forget the time when Big Tim came up there; I guess it was hot that day because when he came to me to buy some cookies he was sweating. He had a bald head, so sweat was just glistening on top of it. He took his hand, wiped the sweat from his head, and some of it landed on me. I thought I would just die. I was so mad. I was like, "no hugs from you today, buddy!" I have a thing about other people's sweat. Like, I do *not* want it on me!

Some weekends the ramp would be full. Ms. Johnson would be on the ramp with her table set up. She was the lanyard lady. She made key chains for people. She would also sell lanyards to the children so they could make their own key chains as well as teach them how to do it. Ms. Johnson would do a lot for the community as far as host different events and things of that sort up at the swapmeet. She would have me laughing with that one cigarette hanging from her lips as she made the key chains. I would always think it was going to fall.
 Ms. Johnson also had a gift wrapping booth in the back during the holidays. She was very creative and she loved buying my cookies and cakes. One day we were on the ramp talking about where I grew up, and she said she lived right down the street from me on 59th and Crenshaw. I thought, *what a small world*. My brother and sister knew her too since they were a lot older than me. They knew most of the children on the block.

The guys would all be on the ramp together sometimes, talking freely; you know how guys can get sometimes with their language. Ms. Johnson would give them the look with that cigarette hanging from her mouth and they would apologize. Big Tony and

Sergeant Eric would never come around when she was on the ramp because she would always find something for them to do.

Sometimes the guys would come and stand right up under me and try to talk to me. And I would hate that. I even had one guy try to give me a massage on the ramp; I was like, "No thanks, I'm good." Ms. Johnson would always be watching. She would always tell me to not let them touch me without my permission, and to make them move back if they were too close. She would say, "We're going to have to get you some borders around you so they can keep their distance!"

Ms. Johnson was cool. I knew her son. He would always hit me up for some coffee cakes. He would order whole pans of them. He worked right down the street at their family business, so I didn't mind delivering them. She was the one that told me she liked to put butter on top of the coffee cakes. I thought, *that's too fattening*. I did try it one time and it was good, but like I said, that's adding more calories that I definitely don't need.

Of course we had the brothers on deck from the Nation Of Islam out there, suited and booted with their bow ties on. They'd always be selling bean pies and *Final Call* newspapers.

I'll never forget the time when the brothers were in the parking lot and this car drove by. This guy threw water on one of them, with the rest of the occupants of the car laughing. They thought it was so funny. Baby! Let me tell you, them brothers snatched his ass out of that car so fast my head spun around. They were getting ready to put a beating on him. He was apologizing and everything. Just because them brothers were out there suited and booted, didn't mean you could get it twisted - a lot of them were gang bangers first. They were no punks. It was so funny though. The look on that guy's face when they snatched him out of that car was priceless. I bet he won't throw water on anybody else ever again. I could remember that like it happened yesterday.

    We have this Fruit Of Islam (FOI) brother that comes up there named Fahrenheit. This brother had to have the loudest mouth ever. He be out there preaching to the people. He'd be foaming at the mouth when he talked. But, he was a true hustler. He was on a mission trying to sell them pies and papers. I remember one evening we were all out on the ramp. It was the holiday season and the swapmeet was packed, with everyone selling their goods to the customers. Brother Fahrenheit was on deck with everyone else. But of course, he was the loudest. Brother Fahrenheit was suited and booted with his brimmed hat on. Baby! I'm telling you, he was fired up out there preaching that word, honey! This brother never got tired. Sometimes other brothers would go to a different ramp and just let him have that one. You have to visualize in your mind that this brother was out there on the ramp day after day with that loud voice, preaching to the people while selling his bean pies and papers. He was out there making money too. One day, a car pulled up in the middle of the crosswalk. People looked at them, wondering why they decided to stop there.

Guess who got out of the car? Brother Fahrenheit's baby mamma! She started yelling at him, "Where is my child support, you sorry MF? You out here preaching to these people and you know your ass don't even take care of your own children!" She added, "You selling all these pies and papers and your children are getting nothing from it!" I've never seen this brother so quiet before. The whole ramp stopped what they were doing to listen to the conversation. Then she hopped back in the car and took off. That brother was so silent. I believe he left early that day.

Clyde, Melvin, Derrick, and myself just started to laugh. Of course Clyde and Melvin had jokes. Clyde was like, "What? You ain't taking care of your kids, my brother?" Melvin was like, "Damn! This nigga feeling embarrassed like a mutha!" Then Melvin would laugh. Derrick just looked, laughed, and shook his head. The baby mama shut him down for the day. Even though he did try to argue back with her for a minute, she was way louder than he was. The other brothers were shaking their heads, saying things like, "Brother, you ain't taking care of the children out here by representing the NOI. I know FOI was going to get him straight. Sometimes I think we need to clean up our own lives up before we try to help someone else. His hypocrisy came back to bite him.

However, I did commend the FOIs out there in the streets, especially at the Slauson Swapmeet, trying to enlighten the mindsets of our people. It's a hard job. And those brothers be out there religiously. Even though they got cussed out a lot, they managed to soldier through it all. I remember when my mother used to take me to see the Honorable Minister Louis Farrakhan speak back in the day. I enjoyed listening to him. My mother would get all the latest tapes of him speaking and bring them for the family to listen to when we went to our second home in Georgia. She had a friend in the Nation that she would get the tapes from. They would all be gathered in the family room listening to him speak, fired up to hear the truth he had to say.

I started going to the mosque as well. I really learned a lot, especially about the condition of our people and what needed to be done. It really changed my life as far as my thought process went. I viewed things differently. My eating habits changed after reading the book, *How to Eat to Live* by the Honorable Elijah Muhammad, PBUH. I felt so much better when I would pray and fast. I'm far from perfect, but I do try to better myself every day. And I would love to hear Minister Tony speak. He was always on point with that knowledge and such a comedian. He would have me rolling.

On a different note, let me tell you about this older lady, Ms. Ruth. She had to be about seventy years old. She used to come up to the swapmeet with her son. She had a nice Cadillac that her son was always driving. She would always ride in the passenger side with a cup in her hands. And we all knew what was in that cup. We knew she was a heavy drinker. She was a very nice and truthful person, though. She would have us laughing so hard on the ramp.

One time she decided to help me sell cookies. Ms. Ruth would encourage those passing by, "Come on baby and buy some of these cookies!" She would always get other people to buy them. Then there would be the ladies that said, "No thank you, I'm trying to watch my weight." Ms. Ruth would reply, "You don't look like you missing any meals to me!" Then she would turn to Derrick and I and whisper, "With her fat ass!" That would definitely be the liquor talking. I didn't want this lady helping me sell my cookies and cakes, but she insisted.

Another time Ms. Ruth came up there to the Swapmeet and her son dropped her off right in front again. He left her and went to the car wash. I'm pretty sure she told him to drop her off all the time so she could come visit us. One day she crept up the ramp, slightly tilted to the side and wanted to sit down in one of my chairs. The next thing we knew, Ms. Ruth fell over from being drunk with liquor and rolled down the ramp, landing next to the brother selling the papers. He didn't know what to do; it happened so fast. We all ran over to her and tried to help her up off the ground. She got up and said, "I'm alright! Shit, I've had harder falls than this." Derrick and I just laughed inside. Our souls were tickled pink. The brother with the pies just looked at me and shook his head. By that time her son had come to pick her up. I'm pretty sure he would have been glad to miss the embarrassing moment we just witnessed. And of course after she left, we all laughed out loud, and were glad she didn't hurt herself.

Another time, she came up there with her son and he left her on the ramp again. I'm assuming that she didn't tell him about the fall she had last time. He went into the swapmeet to do some shopping and this time she decided to stand up next to me. Here we go again. This time Derrick wasn't there, but the brother with the pies was. Once again she lost her balance and down she went. This time she was so close to me she almost took me with her! We helped her back up again and this time I fussed at her. I told her this ramp was not a safe place for her to wait for her son. She told me she was used to falling down and she'd be fine. This lady was stubborn; you couldn't tell her anything. When her son came out, I told him what happened and he said she was always falling. I was like, "You don't think that's a problem?" He responded, "She'll be alright." I'm like, *Lord have mercy on her soul and please don't let her come back*.

I remember she told me that her old man was in jail for life. Ms. Ruth said back in the day she was something else and I believe her. I thought to myself, *She is still something else*. I haven't seen her in a while. The last time we talked she said she couldn't come up here anymore. Our prayers were answered, because I really didn't want her to hurt herself. Ms Ruth did say she was on parole. I asked her why. She said she was on parole for a GTA. "Isn't that Grand Theft Auto?" I replied. She looked at me and smiled. After that I didn't ask any more questions. She told me she drank and smoked weed. I could just imagine what her and her husband were doing back in the day. God bless her; she's alright with me.

Meanwhile, Derrick had given me some good news. He had found love. The young lady he'd been dating had finally stolen his heart and they planned to go to Vegas and get married. I was so happy for my brother. He deserved a good woman. And in the meantime here came Clyde pulling his suitcase. He had been on the down low for a while. He would just walk around with a black bag full of movies but never wanted to set up. Soon as the people spotted him, they rushed up to him.

We were all just chilling on the ramp with Derrick telling Clyde about his good news. Clyde was happy for him as well. Next thing you know, Derrick got a call on the radio and off he went. Apparently there was a gang fight inside. Next thing you knew, people started running out of the swapmeet. I had to move my cookies and cakes to the side. I didn't want them getting trampled over.

Next thing I knew, the gang bangers ran outside every which way. The security team was right behind them. Once I saw them run to their cars, I knew I needed to run for cover, because they always start shooting. Suddenly, customers were running everywhere, screaming. *Bang! Bang! Bang!* was all you could hear. One of the guys get shot. I don't know if the security shot him or one of the gang members shot him, but he was hurt nonetheless. By the time the police came they had already escaped.

I could see the tired look on Derrick's face when he came back. He said, "I'm tired of this shit. I need a new job." I'm thinking, *here we go again with this 'needing a new job' crap*. I told him, "You're about to get married! You can't quit now!" Then he decided to tell me his girlfriend was pregnant. I was like, "Oh! *That's* why you're getting married so fast." He looked at me and smiled. I told him to put in applications for other places while still working security.

Eventually, they ended up getting married and his wife gave birth to twins. Derrick's hands were full and his pockets were empty if you know what I mean. That was a very expensive life change for him. Sometimes I think being by yourself is not so bad. I thought this especially because he would always tell his little sister about his problems. He encouraged me to stay single. Ha! Even though I knew I had my own share of problems dealing with my significant other.

Through it all, Derrick remained at the Slauson. His marriage stayed rocky and the babies kept coming. He always liked sports, so he had his own team after a while if you know what I mean. At least he wasn't lonely anymore. He had a crazy wife and a house full of children.

Marriages

Marriages and relationships were always rocky with all the guys. Maybe because they worked those long hours and it put a strain on their relationships. I was always the ear that listened and never judged. Like Clyde and Melvin. They eventually went back to their wives. Or should I say, the wives *let them* come back home.

Melvin surprisingly came back to work for Diamond Security for a short time. Melvin and Clyde used to both work for the company years ago. Melvin said he was tired of chasing women and therefore wanted to be more responsible and productive with his time. He said he was going to stay with his wife and children and take initiative by working hard every day to keep them happy. That is, until the next big butt came walking by.

Clyde said he couldn't work for anybody else. He insisted on being his own boss. His wife would come up to the swapmeet with the children asking for money, so everything was back to normal. I hadn't seen Brenda and Sheila, their ex-girlfriends, in months. I guess their money train had come to a halt, now that the wives were back in the picture. Clyde would still be telling jokes.

Clyde also had a new friend that he would bring with him. He said he met him at the coffee shop. His name was Dan. Dan looked like a bum. His clothes were always dirty and his teeth were missing in the front. Clyde probably felt sorry for him and took him in. Clyde liked to joke around a lot but he had a big heart. Even though he talked about this man like a dog. But, that was his new roll dog.

Clyde said that Dan was in the middle of a lawsuit. He was suing LAUSD for the fifth time. Once he said that, Dan started talking. He became really heated and got right up in my face to tell me why he was suing them and I felt spit hit me. I had to back away quick. I don't do spit. Since Dan had been coming up there every weekend, he became very comfortable with us. He talked *way* too much.

Clyde eventually got him to help sell movies too. Dan always loved to talk about food and what he ate that day. So, I guess Clyde was feeding him well. I think he even stayed with Clyde and his family sometimes. Dan loved to say he acted like a pit bull when it came to the money he claimed the school board owed him. He seemed to be like an intelligent dummy. He was very smart but didn't have common sense. Clyde was always pointing this out. Sometimes I thought Clyde was Fred from *Sanford and Son*, because he was always calling him 'dummy.' Clyde said he was always doing stupid stuff.

I liked to watch Dan go up to people on the ramp and talk to them, plus see their facial expressions when he showered them with his spray of spit. They'd move back quick because they weren't expecting it, just like I wasn't. It was so funny to me; sometimes I just laughed to myself before it would happen. I never realized how important teeth were. I guess that's why we need them - to hold saliva in your mouth when you talk. Dan was missing several teeth and the ones that were still in there were barely holding on. Everybody that hung out with Clyde was funny to me.

Another day on the ramp, and Clyde, Dan, Derrick, and Captain Tony were all out there with me. Of course Clyde was cracking jokes. He saw Dan looking at this woman. Clyde said, "This nigga Dan might be slow, but he hasn't forgotten about that woman." And Dan would reply, "I haven't had a woman since World War 3." And then he would laugh. I'd just be shaking my head, looking at the Captain. And he'd look back at me and shake his head as well. Then Dan would start toward Tony to talk and he'd be like, *time to go.* So Captain Tony would leave the ramp.

Getting back to relationships, Captain Tony couldn't wait to get out of his. He had been married for years with his fine self but was not happy. He seemed like a good man willing to stay in his marriage, at least until the children got out of school. I couldn't imagine making him miserable. If I was his wife, those meals would be cooked *every day*. He would come home to a nice massage and all of that. But, sometimes you never know. You might think a guy is good because you know him from work, but to actually live with them is a different story. All I know is if my husband was that fine, we would go to counseling or something.

And then there was Eric, the sergeant; he had several women, so you knew he was happy. He was living like a king. I could never figure out how he kept up with all of them. But, eventually life catches up to you. He was this one guy I admired - he was always so clean and neatly dressed. The cars he drove were always nice, like straight off of a show room floor. He would always keep the officers in check. He made sure their uniforms were nice and neat. All the vendors trusted him. He would run a thief down to get back merchandise. I always thought he should have been a sheriff officer. He was very professional.

But, baby, let me tell you, one weekend I didn't see him and I wondered if he decided to take a vacation. They said he was on a permanent vacation. I'm like, "What the hell?" They said he was let go. So, I had to ask what happened because he seemed damn near perfect to me. So, the word on the street was that he was stealing from the vendors for years. Honey, when they told me that, I damn near fell out my chair and rolled down the ramp like Ms. Ruth. I could not believe what I was hearing. I thought to myself, *was it all a facade, while he did his dirt for all those years? No wonder he always looked like a million bucks! He paid himself well.* But you know for years the Koreans made millions of dollars off black folks. I remember this one Korean family had their teenagers driving a Lexus to school. I'm pretty sure they all did, but I just remembered this particular family. The daughter even wrecked the car one night coming from the club. Our children, on the other hand, had to catch the bus, poor as hell. 1I said all of that to say maybe he saw what I saw and wanted better for his children, too. It didn't make it right, though.

As the months went by, we saw less and less of Clyde. Dan eventually moved back in with his ex-girlfriend, so Clyde didn't have anyone to sell the movies with anymore. Clyde then started working at a car dealership. He was doing pretty good selling cars. Then he ended up getting sick from his diabetes, so he struggled for years and eventually died. It was so sad. I didn't get to say goodbye. Soon after he died, I had a dream. And in the dream I was walking somewhere and there was a crowd of people in front of me. One of those people was Clyde. He turned around and waved at me. I knew that was him saying goodbye. I will truly miss him because I know there is no one that can make me laugh like he did. R.I.P. my brother.

Now Lawrence, the security officer with the bunions, ended up getting sick as well, so he stopped working for the security company. Lawrence and I were born on the same day, July 4th. We were like two of a kind. He was diagnosed with breast cancer. That's when I learned men could get breast cancer too. He put up a good fight for a long time. He beat it once, but it came back. He ended up dying. I went to see him at the hospital during his last days on earth. That really hurt my heart to see him like that. He was a good brother and we all miss him. R.I.P. my brother.

James left the security team and started driving trucks. He never got married or had any children. We would talk on the phone from time to time but we never went out. He would also come up to the swapmeet to see everybody. Whenever I pass by a Piggly Wiggly grocery store in the south I always think about him. He would always make jokes about it. Well, James ended up getting sick and he died as well. Another good man gone too soon. R.I.P. James; we had a lot of fun together on the ramp. I will miss him.

Derrick ended up getting a divorce. I wasn't surprised, because his wife acted like she didn't trust him. And they argued all the time. So, I knew that was coming. His ex-wife found someone else quickly after. They would come up to the swapmeet together. I would just look and smile, thinking to myself, *Damn, she got a man already*. He married her with all those children, so he had to be a pretty good man. Derrick never had too much to say. I guess he was just glad to be free. Derrick found himself a young Latina woman. I guess after that, he wasn't fooling around with the sistas anymore.

Derrick finally left the security company after all those years of saying he wanted out. I was proud of him. He moved to Vegas and got a good job. He would still come back and forth for his children. Sometimes he would come up to the swapmeet when he was in town. He said he was happy with his life and I was happy for him.
Big Tony the captain finally got his divorce. He was on countdown, waiting for his children to graduate from high school. He was a good man in my book. He stayed and waited for his children to graduate before he left. Most men don't do that. But he is happy and free now. I can just imagine him going through that pocket of numbers he had over the years (just kidding). But, I know it didn't take him long to find someone.

Switching Lanes

As for me, the "Cookie Lady," I decided to switch lanes and do something different. I moved to Atlanta and started another business called "Nazree's Essence Of A Queen" (nazrees.com). I'm into fragrances now. We have an array of different scents for the body and the house. I also whip the fragrances into shea body butters. I have a lot of natural oils as well for the hair and skin. This is definitely my second love aside from baking. I had move to be closer to Momma Rosa since Atlanta was where she retired and moved to.

  I spent so many years at the Slauson Swapmeet. I bonded with all the security team; they were like part of my family. They all hold a special place in my heart. I also met a lot of people from all over the place. I had so much fun over the years sharing my baked goods with so many people and engaging in conversation with them. From dodging bullets by hiding behind cars to almost laughing my guts out every weekend, I wouldn't trade those experiences for anything. I enjoyed (almost) everyone's company. I have so much more to write about, but I thought this was a good start. I love all the people that have supported me throughout the years. I want to send a special shout-out to Mr. T for allowing me to sell my cookies and cakes at the swapmeet over the years. I also want to thank my team at home, my children, Jennifer, Jessica and Rashad for loading the boxes of cookies and cakes to the truck every weekend. And sometimes they would help me at the swapmeet sell the bake goods, while I went home to back some more. They were born into the business. So, they enjoyed eating their moms pastries over the years. I also wanted to acknowledge all my friends, coworkers, and security officers at the Slauson Swapmeet for always brightening my day and filling it with encouragement and support. We lost so many of you, but I wanted to mention just how much I appreciated you guys and cherished the time we spent together. It didn't go unnoticed. Rest in peace.

    My decision to leave the Slauson swapmeet was tough. I thought, *I'm really going to miss this place that I've grown to love over the years.* The excitement of seeing all the people coming to shop and buy cookies and cakes. The thrill of watching Slauson's finest Diamond Security in action. The love and support that the community gave me. The long talks and advice I gave to people that needed it. I was scared to leave it all behind and move on to my next venture in life.

There were so many things going on in my family that was pulling me toward a life in the south. Momma Rosa had retired years ago and moved to Georgia, so she needed me to move and be closer to where she was at. Deep down inside I knew the love of the Slauson Swapmeet would eventually call me back.

That's why I decided to write this book. "Cookie Lady" is back. Back to the world that embraces my spirit and makes my heart sing to the melody of freshly baked cookies and cake.

www.ingramcontent.com/pod-product-compliance
Lightning Source LLC
Chambersburg PA
CBHW030158100526
44592CB00009B/338